WORKING TOWARD ACHIEVING
WORKERS' RIGHTS

Catherine Brereton

CRABTREE
PUBLISHING COMPANY
WWW.CRABTREEBOOKS.COM

CRABTREE
PUBLISHING COMPANY
WWW.CRABTREEBOOKS.COM

Author: Catherine Brereton
Picture Manager: Sophie Mortimer
Designer: Lynne Lennon
Design Manager: Keith Davis
Children's Publisher: Anne O'Daly
Editorial director: Kathy Middleton
Editor: Janine Deschenes
Proofreader: Wendy Scavuzzo
Print coordinator: Katherine Berti

Copyright © Brown Bear
Books Ltd 2020

Photographs: (t=top, b= bottom, l=left, r=right, c=center)

Front Cover: Alamy: Enigma (bottom left); Shutterstock: Atomazul (right), Robert J Daveant (bottom center); Wikimedia Commons: Library of Congress (center left)

Interior: Alamy: agencia FORUM 31t, The Granger Collection 6, Niday Picture Library 15, Trinity Mirror/Mirrorpix 24–25, World History Archive 34; Brown Bear Books: 23; Debasers Filums Ltd: 35; Dreamstime: Tomasz Bidermann 36, Sheila Fitzgerald 29, Marcin Kadziolka 33, Monkey Business Images 7t; Getty Images: Bettmann 19t, Francis Miller 11, Cathy Murphy 22, Scot Olson 28, Jim Wilkes 26; iStock: 32; Library of Congress: 20; Public Domain: Bryant & May 14, S Liles/Southern Hollows 18; Shutterstock: adirekjog 7r, Stanislav Beloglazov 17, Everett Collection 16, Iakov Filimonov 10, Ben Gengell 5b, Watchares Hansawek 37, S.K Hassan Ali 38, HomeArt 24 A Katz 5t, 21, Olekander Marynchenko 13b, Emilja Mijkovic 4, Graham Montanri 19b, Nicku 8, Tatiana Popov 31b, rbifmr 27, Matyas Rehak 30, Summerlee Schmitt 1, 9; U.S. Government Cornell Education 13t, International Ladies Garment Workers Union Archives, Kheel Center Collection, Cornell University 12.

Brown Bear Books has made every attempt to contact the copyright holder. If you have any information about omissions, please contact licensing@brownbearbooks.co.uk

Library and Archives Canada Cataloging in Publication

Title: Working toward achieving workers' rights / Catherine Brereton.
Names: Brereton, Catherine, author.
Description: Series statement: Achieving social change | Includes bibliographical references and index.
Identifiers: Canadiana (print) 2020029931X | Canadiana (ebook) 20200299417 | ISBN 9780778779506 (softcover) | ISBN 9780778779445 (hardcover) | ISBN 9781427125484 (HTML)
Subjects: LCSH: Labor movement—Juvenile literature. | LCSH: Labor unions—Juvenile literature. | LCSH: Civil rights—Juvenile literature. | LCSH: Employee rights—Juvenile literature. | LCSH: Labor laws and legislation—Juvenile literature.
Classification: LCC HD4902.5 .B74 2021 | DDC j331.88—dc23

Library of Congress Cataloging-in-Publication Data

Names: Brereton, Catherine, author.
Title: Working toward achieving workers' rights / Catherine Brereton.
Description: New York : Crabtree Publishing Company, 2021. | Series: Achieving social change | Includes bibliographical references and index.
Identifiers: LCCN 2020032438 (print) | LCCN 2020032439 (ebook) | ISBN 9780778779445 (hardcover) | ISBN 9780778779506 (paperback) | ISBN 9781427125484 (ebook)
Subjects: LCSH: Employee rights--Juvenile literature. | Labor movement--Juvenile literature. | Sex discrimination in employment--Juvenile literature.
Classification: LCC HD6971.8 .B74 2021 (print) | LCC HD6971.8 (ebook) | DDC 331.01/1--dc23
LC record available at https://lccn.loc.gov/2020032438
LC ebook record available at https://lccn.loc.gov/2020032439

Crabtree Publishing Company
www.crabtreebooks.com   1-800-387-7650

Published in Canada
Crabtree Publishing
616 Welland Ave.
St. Catharines, ON
L2M 5V6

Published in the United States
Crabtree Publishing
347 Fifth Ave
Suite 1402-145
New York, NY 10016

Published by CRABTREE PUBLISHING COMPANY in 2021

Printed in the U.S.A./092020/CG20200810

CONTENTS

INTRODUCTION

All over the world, every day and night, millions of people are working—making things, farming, selling things, building, writing, cleaning, caring for others, teaching, and more. They make up the world's workforce.

When people work, they expect to be paid. They are exchanging their effort, time, and skills for the money they need to survive and support their families. They expect to be safe. They expect to have time off, such as in the evenings, on weekends, and some holidays.

Workers have not always had these rights. Around the world, many don't have these rights even today, or laws protecting these rights are broken. Even in the richest countries, there are groups of workers who are paid badly or treated less fairly. Throughout history, workers have had to fight for their rights—and the battle is never over.

We all depend on the jobs done by millions of different types of workers, such as this grocery store cashier.

In 2014, in New York City and across the world, thousands of fast food workers protested low wages and demanded an increase in the **minimum wage**.

Campaigning for Rights

Activism means campaigning for change. When people decide to stand up for themselves and others, they become activists. Activists may be individuals, or organized groups working together. They protest, go on strike, **boycott**, and call for change. Thanks to their efforts, working conditions have improved. But there is still a long way to go.

Key Events

Wider Struggles

Workers' rights activists have contributed to every **human rights** struggle in history—from the fight for women's right to vote to today's campaign to make the global fashion industry fairer. Workers' rights and human rights go hand in hand. Workers are of different races, genders, religions, and ages. Like all people, they deserve dignity, freedom, and a decent standard of living.

CHAPTER 1

WHAT ARE WORKERS' RIGHTS?

Rights such as the right to work safely, to have a secure job, and to be paid fairly, are relatively new in the history of labor, or work. They are continually changed—by corporations, by governments, and by workers themselves.

Some workers are employed at businesses and organizations. They might be called "staff" or "employees." Most likely, they know what hours they must work and how much they will get paid. They probably have a manager in charge of their work. Other types of workers are called "self-employed," "freelance," or "contractors." They might be hired for individual tasks such as writing a magazine article or driving a taxi. They likely decide their own hours and wages.

*For most of history, workers worked where they lived, like these weavers. Since the **Industrial Revolution**, millions of people go out to work. However, today working at home is on the rise as self-employment becomes more common.*

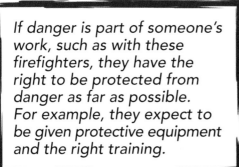

If danger is part of someone's work, such as with these firefighters, they have the right to be protected from danger as far as possible. For example, they expect to be given protective equipment and the right training.

Fair Pay, Fair Hours, and Safety

All kinds of workers have the right to be paid a fair amount for their work. They have the right to work a maximum number of hours. But this only applies to one job. If people have several jobs, or are freelance workers, they may end up working extremely long hours. People also have the right to work in a safe environment. However, for much of history, corporations faced no penalty if their workers were injured or even killed. Workers' rights activists changed this.

Key Events

Celebrating Workers

Labor Day is a holiday that celebrates workers and everything they do to make a country strong and successful. It began in 1882, and falls on the first Monday in September in the United States and Canada. International Workers' Day or May Day (May 1) honors workers' struggles and is celebrated around the world.

What Is Labor?

The word labor means people's work—effort, time, and skills—or working people as a group or class. In society, workers don't always get a fair deal, but there is strength in numbers.

Workers are vital to a company or country's strength and success. Their labor creates wealth, but they don't usually get a big share of that wealth. Employers and business leaders are paid very large amounts, sometimes hundreds of times what the ordinary workers are paid. This is pay inequality, and today the gap is getting wider.

Karl Marx wrote about labor in society. His theories have influenced political thinkers of many different kinds ever since.

Key Voices

Karl Marx

In the 19th century, Karl Marx observed that in the system called **capitalism**, most of the money and power belongs to corporations and the government, which he called the ruling class. The working class sells their labor and creates wealth for others, but does not have power or control. He wanted to build a new kind of society in which everyone was equal, and where workers were more in control.

In 2019, teaching unions in Chicago went on strike. They won a pay increase and the promise of more nurses, social workers, and librarians to support them.

Getting Organized

When workers get together, this is known as organized labor. It happens through groups called labor unions or **trade unions**. Trade unions are generally made up of workers who do a particular job. There are unions for farm workers, teachers, nurses, and electricians, for example. Today, more than 176 million people worldwide are members of a labor union, creating strength in numbers.

Members of a trade union campaign to protect each other. They do this by talking with employers and agreeing on rules about things such as pay, hours, safety, and health care and retirement benefits. This is called collective bargaining. Union activists put pressure on companies and lawmakers, always trying to improve things for workers.

Righting Wrongs

Throughout history, workers have been subjected to low pay, poor job security, and dangerous conditions. Labor activists have taken up the challenge to set things right.

In 1900s America, for example, clothing-factory workers would often be fined half a day's pay for being a few minutes late, or for pricking their fingers and getting blood on the cloth. This meant they were not paid for all of their labor. Working on the railroad, meanwhile, was so dangerous that it was common to lose a hand, or a leg, and one out of every 117 workers died on the job. Sadly, unsafe workplaces aren't just for the history books. Today, there are dangerous conditions in fashion factories worldwide.

Sandblasting denim gives it a faded look, but can be deadly. From 2005 to 2007, at least 42 workers in Turkey died from lung disease caused by sandblasting denim.

Key Events

The Winnipeg General Strike of 1919

The Winnipeg General Strike of 1919 was the largest strike in Canadian history. As workers in the city struggled with poverty after World War I (1914–1918), they attempted to **negotiate** better pay and better working conditions. More than 30,000 factory, city, and transit workers stopped work. It helped unite working class Canadians and spark more activism across the country.

Demanding Change

All through the 20th century, labor activists fought for better pay, reasonable hours, and safe conditions. Activists use various **tactics** to press for change. They come up with proposals and demands for employers to agree to or for governments to make laws about. If their demands are ignored, one option is for the workers to go on strike. This means they refuse to go to work until their demands are met. This is not an easy decision, because striking workers don't get paid, and they may lose their jobs altogether. But many of the workers' rights we take for granted have been won through the actions of strikers.

The steel strike of 1959 was the largest work stoppage in American history. Factories all over the United States stood empty and quiet for nearly four months as workers stopped work to campaign for better pay. These workers played catch outside while on strike.

CHAPTER 2

SAFETY AT WORK

In March 1911, a terrible fire at the Triangle Shirtwaist Factory in New York City killed 146 people and shocked the nation.

It was Saturday. The factory workers were getting ready to go home, excited to start the weekend. When fire broke out, they raced to get out of the building. One exit was locked and the fire escape collapsed with people on it. It was a picture of horror.

The Triangle was one of over 450 clothing factories in Manhattan. Many of its workers were young women from **immigrant** backgrounds. It was thought of as a modern, efficient factory, but workers had to put up with low pay, long hours, and dangerous conditions. In 1909, there was a strike, led by Clara Lemlich and made up of members of the International Ladies' Garment Workers' Union (ILGWU). But the Triangle owners had ignored workers' calls for safety improvements.

In 1909, Clara Lemlich was only 23 years old, but she was determined to stick up for her fellow workers and led a strike of thousands of women and girls.

> The fire crept closer to us and we were crowded at the elevator door banging and hollering.
>
> Celia Walker Friedman, fire survivor

Firefighters sped to the scene, but their ladders were not long enough to reach the factory, high on the 8th to 10th floors.

The Trial and Aftermath

In December 1911, factory owners Max Blanck and Isaac Harris went on trial, accused of causing the workers' deaths. Witnesses told of large garbage cans filled with cotton scraps, which caught fire easily. A fire bucket, which should have contained water or sand, had been empty. All but one exit was locked. People all over the nation were shocked by what they read about the trial in newspapers. Unions distributed money to help victims' families and survivors. They demanded action to improve the unsafe conditions.

Exposing Dangers at Work

The Triangle tragedy sparked calls for reforms to make factories safer. Elsewhere, other terrible situations prompted activists to tackle dangerous working conditions.

After the fire, activists from the ILGWU stepped up efforts to organize workers. Together with other reform groups, they sent out a questionnaire to find out what dangers needed to be dealt with, and pushed for new safety rules. The city made fireproof stairwells, fire alarms, and fire extinguishers mandatory. These safety standards set an example for the rest of the United States.

Improvements often took time. In London, U.K., in 1888, girls in a match factory went on strike. A dangerous chemical was causing a disease in their jaws. Factory employers were quick to agree to the girls' demands on fines and pay, but were slow on safety. It was 13 years before the factory stopped using the chemical and more than 20 years before it was banned.

The match girls proved that even though they were very poor, very young, and girls, they could do something useful to help themselves when they worked together.

The Radium Girls

Some work can cause serious or even fatal illness, but this can be hard to prove. "Radium girls" hand-painted military dials with glow-in-the-dark **radioactive** paint. They even licked the brushes. They were told the paint was safe, although chemists working with it used protective screens and masks. Workers suffered horrific illnesses, and many died. Some teamed up with lawyers to fight and, in 1938, their employer was found responsible. The case led to life-saving rules, such as the compulsory use of protective equipment to protect workers.

"Radium girls" painted the numbers and hands of clock dials with highly radioactive paint. They were given no warnings or protections.

Key Events

Safety Laws

The radium girls' case helped pave the way for the 1970 Occupational Safety and Health Act. Before this, 14,000 people died at work in the United States every year. In 2017, it was around 5,000. Laws protect workers from dangers such as noise, dangerous chemicals, unsafe machines, and more.

Children at Work

Many workers in the Triangle Shirtwaist Factory and the London match factory were less than 16 years old. They were part of a vast army of working children at the time.

Children have worked for most of history, helping with farming and domestic tasks. But the Industrial Revolution meant child labor jumped in scale. Huge numbers of factories grew up, drawing in thousands of people to do all the jobs inside. Children had nimble fingers and could fit into tiny spaces—and they could be paid less. Poor children as young as four years of age worked in coal mines, as chimney sweeps, in mills, and selling newspapers in the street. They worked long hours, in dangerous conditions, received little or no education, and had little time to play.

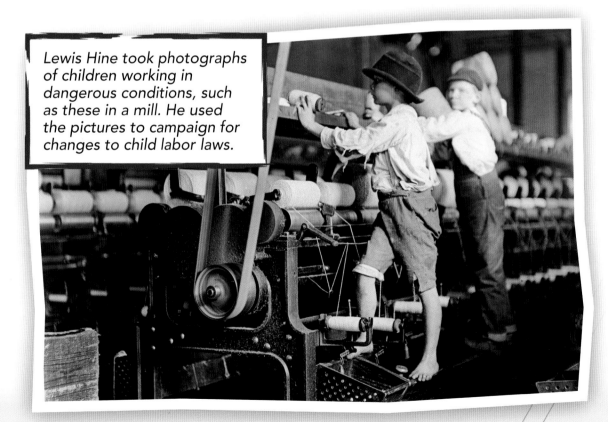

Lewis Hine took photographs of children working in dangerous conditions, such as these in a mill. He used the pictures to campaign for changes to child labor laws.

Many people campaigned to make life better for child workers. Authors, such as Charles Dickens, told stories and photographers, including Lewis Hine, took pictures that brought the desperate situation of child workers to public attention.

Tackling Child Labor

Campaigners put pressure on lawmakers and, from the 1830s, laws were passed reducing the number of hours children could work. In 1938, the U.S. Fair Labor Standards Act made it illegal to employ children under 14. In Canada, most provinces had outlawed work by children under 14 by 1929. Today, around 152 million kids are in child labor. Of these, about 72 million are in hazardous work.

Children like this girl carrying bricks in a factory in Nepal have to work because of poverty. Their families rely on income from their children's labor.

Key Events

Children on Strike

Sometimes, child workers themselves took a stand. An example was the New York newsboys' strike of 1899. There was a price increase for newspaper-sellers buying their newspapers to sell, so the youngsters went on strike. They won a better deal.

CHAPTER 3

POWER FOR THE OPPRESSED

In February 1968, sanitation workers in Memphis, Tennessee, went on strike. The mostly Black workers were fed up with being treated as if they were worth nothing.

It was a bleak, wintry day. Around 1,300 sanitation workers were fed up. Only days before, workers Echol Cole and Robert Walker had been killed at work, crushed to death by a faulty garbage truck while trying to shelter from the rain. Life was hard for the sanitation workers. They drove garbage trucks and had to lift heavy, leaking, unsanitary garbage. They had no protective clothing and no place to wash up. Their wages were not enough for them to live on, and many were forced to rely on **welfare**. New mayor Henry Loeb refused to pay **overtime** for night shifts.

The garbage truck that killed Cole and Walker looked like this one. Mayor Loeb had refused to replace old, worn-out trucks, putting the workers at risk.

Mayor Loeb called in heavily armed troops, providing an intimidating escort for the sanitation workers as they marched in peaceful protest.

Support and Dignity

In Memphis, Black citizens had long suffered lower pay, exclusion from labor unions, and violent treatment from the police. Before the strike, the sanitation workers had little support from the wider community. But that changed. The strikers unionized and were backed by large labor unions and the National Association for the Advancement of Colored People (NAACP). When police used mace and tear gas against nonviolent demonstrators, people were shocked into standing alongside the strikers. Every day during the strike, strikers met at noon and marched from a church to downtown. Local high school and college students—many of them White—marched with them. Black churchgoers donated food to the strikers. Workers carried signs that read "I AM A MAN." The protest was about more than improvements to pay and safety. It was about human dignity.

> ... if you stand up straight, people can't ride your back. And that's what we did. We stood up straight.
> Taylor Rogers, striker

A Wider Struggle

The sanitation workers' strike was part of a wider struggle for civil rights. **In the face of injustice, Black workers were standing up for their right to be treated decently and fairly.**

Memphis minister Rev. James Lawson realized that the poor treatment of the sanitation workers echoed the treatment of Black people throughout America. Lawson invited civil rights leader Martin Luther King, Jr. to address the strikers in March. King praised the labor activists and churchgoers for their **solidarity** and unity. He told them it was important for Black people to stand together.

Demonstrators in the March on Washington in 1963 included church groups, labor organizations, civil rights groups, and public figures.

Key Events

March on Washington for Jobs and Freedom

In 1963, more than 250,000 demonstrators took part in a march for equal civil rights for Black people. Martin Luther King, Jr. addressed the crowds. Together, they protested inequalities and injustices faced by Black communities, such as lower wages, poorer job prospects, and a higher likelihood of being unemployed.

Together, they could pressure the city of Memphis to treat the sanitation workers fairly. The following evening, King was assassinated. Lawson urged citizens to stay calm, and ministers finally persuaded the mayor to agree to the strikers' demands.

Union Power

The sanitation workers' strike showed the power of labor unions. Before the strike began, few of the sanitation workers belonged to a union. They had even been fired for trying to do so. But once they joined the American Federation of State, County and Municipal Employees (AFSCME)—which was actively recruiting, or hiring, Black workers in the 1960s—they had strength and support.

Racism including police brutality is still an urgent problem. Activist groups such as Black Lives Matter campaign for reforms that end violence against Black people and push for equal opportunities for them.

Unions in Action

The Memphis example shows how labor activism can have real power for change. Unions harness this power in different ways. They use many tactics to achieve change.

Headline-hitting strikes are perhaps the best-known tactic that unions have. However, it doesn't always take a strike for unions to campaign for better conditions. They do it everywhere, all the time. In many companies, unions have recognition. This means the employer has formally agreed to work with a particular union, and negotiate on pay and other conditions. The workers are in a strong bargaining position. Even where unions are not recognized, unions put pressure on governments to make laws that help workers.

César Chávez and Dolores Huerta co-founded the National Farm Workers Association and inspired activists all over the world.

Farm Labor Rights

Starting in 1965, grape pickers in Delano, California, went on strike. Grape pickers were often **migrants**, who had fewer rights than other workers. They included **Latino** and **Filipino** migrants. Strike leaders César Chávez and Dolores Huerta were both children of Mexican immigrants, and knew how bad things were for migrant workers. The grape pickers worked from dawn to dusk with no breaks, no cold drinking water, and for low wages. Chávez made sure that workers from different countries stuck together. The strikers marched 250 miles (400 km) to Sacramento. They asked members of the public to stop buying grapes. This tactic is called a boycott. It was successful, and the workers won a new contract with better pay and health benefits.

As thousands of farm workers marched, they told people about their conditions and gained public support.

Key Voices

Industrial Workers of the World

Many unions were open to specific groups of workers only. The Industrial Workers of the World (IWW), nicknamed "the Wobblies," formed in 1905. They wanted to create one big union for all workers, especially unskilled workers from various disadvantaged groups. They were a powerful force, with hundreds of thousands of members.

CHAPTER 4

FAIR PAY FOR WOMEN

In June 1968, a walkout by women workers at the Ford car factory in Dagenham, United Kingdom, put the issue of unequal pay for women firmly on the agenda.

The women were angry that their pay had just been cut. The different jobs in the factory had been reclassified, and theirs—sewing covers for car seats—had been classed as unskilled, and put on a lower pay grade than some other jobs in the factory. These other jobs were done by men, and the strikers were furious, convinced that their skills were valued less just because they were women.

At this time in the United Kingdom, it was legal for women to be paid less than men. At first, the Ford strikers were not protesting the pay inequality. They simply wanted their work to be recognized as just as skilled as the men's work. Their action brought the factory to a standstill.

> If you feel that you're not being treated fairly, you have got to fight for yourself. Go for it girl!
> Gwen Davis and Eileen Pullen, strikers

Standing Together

The 187 strikers had support from many of their male colleagues, along with 197 women at another Ford factory who walked out in solidarity. Their action hit the headlines as the women walked to Parliament, waving their banners. They were determined to stand up for what was right. Barbara Castle, the government minister in charge of work, took the women's side. She was already pushing for equal pay for men and women, and the Ford women helped her cause. Over the next few years, momentum built, with activists campaigning for equal pay, and eventually the law was changed.

The strike ended when the women won a pay increase to 92% of the men's wage. It took another strike, in 1984, for their jobs to be classified as skilled.

Women's Pay

The Ford women were just one example of a great wave of activists in the 1970s and 1980s fighting for women's rights to fair pay and fair treatment at work.

At this time, it was usual—and legal—for women to be paid less than men. Women had less opportunity to do certain well-paid jobs or rise up to senior, well-paid positions. In the 1950s and 1960s, there had been a huge increase in the number of women in the workforce, and society was changing. Women wanted a fairer deal at work. In workplaces and labor organizations everywhere, activists campaigned for equal pay. All this pressure was effective. In many countries, the 1960s and 1970s saw new laws ordering equal pay, such as the U.S. Equal Pay Act (1960), the UK Equal Pay Act (1970), and the Canadian Human Rights Act (1977).

Labor activist Grace Hartman was a key figure in the campaign for equal pay in Canada. She chaired the National Action Committee on the Status of Women.

Activists, trade union members, and community leaders protest gender pay inequality on Equal Pay Day.

The Gender Pay Gap

Despite all this, true pay equality didn't happen. It was easy for employers to claim that a job mainly done by men was more skilled, and therefore worth more money, than one done by women. Today, the gender pay gap remains. In the United States in 2019, on average, women earned 79 cents for every dollar earned by men. In Canada in 2019, women earned 84 cents for every dollar earned by men. The gap is even wider for Black, Indigenous, and migrant women, women on low incomes, and women who have disabilities.

Key Events

Equal Pay Day

Equal Pay Day is a symbolic day to raise awareness of the gender pay gap. It varies by year and country. In the United States, it falls on the day that marks how far the average female worker has to work into the next year to earn as much as male workers did the year before. In 2019, the Equal Pay Day was April 2.

A Fairer Workplace

Achieving fair pay for women is only one part of building a fairer and more equal workplace for everyone. Activists work to stamp out many kinds of discrimination **and unfair treatment.**

Working life can be unfair for women in many ways, not just pay. Before the 1980s, paid **maternity leave** was rare. The Canada Post workers' strike of 1981 won postal workers across Canada a trailblazing 17 weeks of paid maternity leave. Activists work to support women with other measures such as protection from being fired for being pregnant, protection from discrimination and sexual harassment, paternity leave, childcare, and more.

Trade union members march on International Women's Day. The event takes place each year on March 8. It grew out of demands for better hours and pay for women workers.

All Kinds of Equality

Workers should have a fair deal no matter what their race, sexual orientation, religion, nationality, or whether they are able-bodied. Sadly, even where laws protect against discrimination, it is common for people to lose job opportunities or be fired because of who they are. And there is a color pay gap like the gender pay gap, too. In the U.S. in 2019, Black men earned an average of 87 cents for every dollar earned by White men.

In 2013, Aimee Stephens was fired from her job when she told her employer she was **transgender**. Stephens took the case to court. In 2019, the U.S. Supreme Court ruled that laws protecting workers from discrimination at work applied to gay and transgender workers—an important victory.

Pride is a celebration of LGBTQ+ people, but it is also a protest. LGBTQ+ people still have to fight for their human rights, including their rights as workers.

CHAPTER 5

ON THE GLOBAL STAGE

In August 1980, amidst a wave of strikes and demonstrations protesting soaring food prices, around 17,000 shipyard workers in the port of Gdańsk, Poland, went on strike.

The strike began when shipyard worker and labor activist Anna Walentynowicz was fired for editing a newspaper that criticized Poland's **Soviet**-backed government. Within days, workers at 200 factories joined in. Soon, representatives from trade unions from across Poland met in Gdańsk and united to form one big independent union, with Lech Wałęsa as leader. The movement was 10 million people strong. It was named Solidarność, which means "solidarity."

This shipyard in the Poland's biggest port, Gdańsk, was the birthplace of a movement that would transform Poland. The flowers are tributes paid in 2016.

Most of Poland's workforce—plus intellectuals, students, priests, and even the Polish-born Pope John Paul II—joined the Solidarność movement.

Solidarność wanted to end the Soviet control of Poland. It also called for free elections and for trade unions to be involved in government decision-making. But the government declared Solidarność illegal, jailed many of its leaders, and even imposed **martial law**. The movement was almost completely crushed by the government's actions.

As the 1980s wore on, the Polish economy stayed weak. In 1988, food prices shot up, there was another wave of strikes, and public support for Solidarność revived. Strikers pushed to participate in free elections, and eventually the government agreed. In June 1989, the polls delivered an incredible victory for the union. An amazing 99 out of 100 seats in the new Senate were won by candidates approved by Solidarność.

> History has taught us that there is no bread without freedom.
> Solidarność

Labor Activism and National Politics

Solidarność was more than a labor organization. In becoming a political party and forming a government, it inspired activists in other eastern European countries.

From the end of World War II, Poland and several other eastern European countries had been under the control of the Soviet Union, or USSR, which was a **communist** state. Communism had grown out of the theories of Karl Marx (see page 8). Communist governments claimed to rule in the interests of the working class. But, in reality, they restricted people's freedoms. This made life in Soviet countries tough. Solidarność's success in Poland was part of a world-changing wave of events in 1989, the most famous of which was the fall of the Berlin Wall.

*The Berlin Wall divided the Soviet-controlled East Berlin from the **democratic** West Berlin. In 1989, crowds of citizens surged through a checkpoint and started to bring down the wall. This event led to a newly united democratic Germany.*

Lech Wałęsa (right) was Poland's first elected president. In 2009, he celebrated 20 years of democracy in Poland, alongside Prime Minister Donald Tusk (later President of the European Council).

Trade Unions and Governments

All around the world, trade unions have played a role in national politics. The Labour Party in Britain, for example, was set up by trade unions to give workers representation in government. Many British trade unions pay money to the party and can help shape its policies. Canada's New Democratic Party (NDP) started in 1961 as the result of a merger between an earlier party, the Co-operative Commonwealth Federation (CCF), and the Canadian Labour Congress (CLC).

Key Voices

Trade Unions and Presidents

Some politicians start as trade union activists. A number of trade union leaders have later become president or prime minister of the country. They include Bob Hawke (Australia 1983–1991), Lula da Silva (Brazil 2003–2011), Jóhanna Sigurðardóttir (Iceland 2009–2013), and Stefan Löfven (Sweden 2014–current).

Workers Uniting Around the World

Strong labor activism inside a country combined with international solidarity and support can be a powerful combination. The anti-apartheid movement in South Africa has shown this.

Apartheid was an unjust system, set up in South Africa in 1948, in which people were **segregated** by race. White people had all the country's power and riches; Black people had few rights of any kind. Activists drove resistance to apartheid. A political party called the African National Congress (ANC) was an important part of the resistance, but it was banned from 1960 to 1990. Several large trade unions of Black workers were key to the long struggle.

The United Democratic Front formed in 1983 to bring together workers, students, churches, and community groups to oppose apartheid. It organized protests including stayaways, where workers refused to go to work.

Workers Against Apartheid

One significant union in the anti-apartheid struggle was the National Union of Mineworkers. Formed by Cyril Ramaphosa in 1982, it pushed to end a system that meant the best-paid jobs were kept for White people. After apartheid, Ramaphosa became a member of parliament and, in 2018, president.

Trade unions and activists all over the world also supported the anti-apartheid movement. There were boycotts of South African goods, and governments imposed **sanctions** on South Africa, which means they would not sell goods or do business there. This international pressure, combined with activists in South Africa never giving up their struggle, resulted in this cruel system ending in the early 1990s.

Global Connections

Workers' actions can have an impact thousands of miles away. In 1973, the world watched in shock when a military **coup** in Chile overthrew the democratic government and its president Salvador Allende. In Scotland, engineers at an aircraft factory refused to repair aircraft engines that had come in from Chile. They knew they would be used to attack the Chilean people. In a show of solidarity, they left the aircraft outside to rust. Their trade union supported their action, and local people in Scotland gave homes to Chilean **refugees**.

THE INCREDIBLE TRUE STORY OF INTERNATIONAL SOLIDARITY

NAE PASARAN!

BAFTA WINNER

BIFA NOMINEE

★★★★
THE HERALD
★★★★
THE FINANCIAL TIMES
★★★★
THE SCOTSMAN
★★★★
THE SKINNY

★★★★
TIME OUT
★★★★
THE NATIONAL
★★★★
EYE FOR FILM
★★★★
THE UPCOMING

"AN EMOTIONALLY-CHARGED JOY TO EXPERIENCE"
THE NATIONAL

"DOCUMENTARY GOLD" "POWERFUL"
THE HERALD   THE GUARDIAN

The story of the Scottish workers was turned into a film, Nae Pasaran. *The title echoes an anti-**fascist** motto, "No pasarán," which means "They shall not pass."*

CHAPTER 6

WORKERS' RIGHTS ACTIVISM TODAY

All over the world, trade unions, along with other activist groups, are campaigning to protect workers. There are also new challenges, including climate change and globalization.

The International Labour Organization (ILO) is part of the United Nations. It is made up of governments, employers, and workers from 187 countries. In 1998, the ILO made a commitment to protect and improve workers' rights in four categories. The first is freedom of association and collective bargaining. This means that workers can form unions and have the power to negotiate. In 107 countries, workers do not have this right, and sometimes labor activists are persecuted. In China in 2019, five labor activists were imprisoned, and 30 striking steelworkers were jailed in Iran.

Amnesty International is a global human rights campaign group. As part of its work, it campaigns for the release of jailed trade union activists.

*In Thailand's fishing industry, **human trafficking** is a problem. Men are forced to work 24-hour shifts to repay debts, and are beaten or killed as punishments.*

Slavery and Child Labor

The second category is elimination of forced labor, which is when work is more like **slavery**. Workers may be forced to work for one employer for years with little or no pay in terrible living conditions. Industries with many workers and few regulations, such as agriculture and fishing, have the most forced labor. The third is abolition of child labor. The ILO is working to eliminate the need for children to work in dangerous conditions or instead of going to school.

Discrimination at Work

The fourth category is elimination of discrimination at work. Many laws and policies protect people against many forms of discrimination. But laws might not cover vulnerable groups, such as migrant workers. The ILO brings together governments, trade unions, employers, and migrant workers' organizations from around the world. It establishes international standards for protecting migrant workers.

Globalization Under the Spotlight

A terrible accident in 2013 echoed the Triangle Shirtwaist Factory fire, showing that despite all that activists have achieved, there is still a long way to go to achieve workers' rights for all.

Today's global fashion industry shows up many of the problems of globalization. Customers worldwide want to buy cheap, fast fashion, and workers in poorer countries often have to work in terrible conditions to make it. In 2013, the world was horrified when the Rana Plaza building in Dhaka, Bangladesh, collapsed, killing more than 1,000 people.

Garment workers in Bangladesh are subject to very low wages, long hours, lack of job security, and dangerous conditions. They are often persecuted for joining trade unions.

FairTrade

FairTrade International campaigns to make life fairer for the workers who grow and produce the items we buy. It works with small businesses that don't have the resources and economic power of big brands. It sets standards such as a minimum price and fair labor conditions.

FairTrade works with producers such as this tea farmer in Kenya to improve working conditions and support community resources such as health care.

The building contained several factories that made clothes for global brands including Mango, Gucci, and Walmart. Workers had noticed and complained about cracks in the building, which was not strong enough for heavy factory machinery, but they were ordered to carry on working.

A Wake-up Call

Fashion brands were criticized for taking little interest in the conditions of the workers who made their clothing. Local activists and international groups, such as Human Rights Watch, got together to support workers' demands for improving safety standards or getting compensation. They campaign for brands to be held responsible when workers are treated badly.

Today's Challenges

In today's globalized world, the challenges facing workers—and labor activists—are changing all the time. There is always a new battle to fight and improvements to be won.

The COVID-19 pandemic has been a major challenge for workers around the world. There were job losses and pay cuts, especially among low-paid workers. Many key workers continued to do their jobs, including health care workers, trash collectors, and delivery workers. Not all were given the right protective clothing or had access to sick pay. In response, activists protested. Workers staged walkouts in Amazon warehouses in New York City, Chicago, and Detroit to highlight safety measures. Unions representing transit workers, including the Amalgamated Transit Union, pushed for hazard pay for workers and for the federal government to set minimum standards for safety equipment.

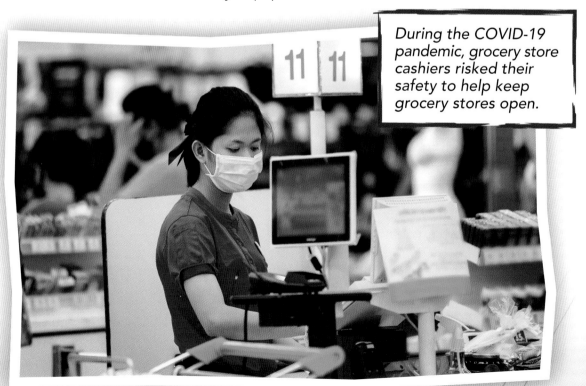

During the COVID-19 pandemic, grocery store cashiers risked their safety to help keep grocery stores open.

Climate Change

One of today's biggest challenges is climate change. Workers are on the front line. Some types of jobs will decline, but the challenge is to move to new, skilled, well-paid jobs in green technologies. Many trade unions are consulting with employers to make workplaces more sustainable. For example, the trade union at a brewery in the UK asked workers at the company for energy-saving ideas. When these were put in place, the company reduced its **carbon footprint** by 40 percent in just two years.

Trade unions around the world supported Greta Thunberg's Global Climate Strike in 2019, including the International Trade Union Confederation, which has 200 million members worldwide.

Key Events

Strike for the Climate

On February 27, 2020, thousands of cleaning workers in Minneapolis walked off work and marched for the environment. Supported by their unions, the workers called for more environmentally friendly cleaning products to be used and training so the cleaners could put green ideas into practice at work.

GET INVOLVED

It's easy to become an activist for workers' rights. Here are some suggestions of how to contribute.

1 Smarter Shopping

Think about the things you buy. Are they made by workers who are treated well? FairTrade is a good place to start for food and fashion.

See www.fairtrade.org. uk/What-is-Fairtrade

2 Boycott

You can take action through what you don't buy as well as what you buy. Boycotting sends a powerful message to the company that you don't approve of it treating workers badly. There is information about boycotts here, or you could start your own:

www.ethicalconsumer.org/ ethicalcampaigns/boycotts

3 Raise Awareness

Learn more about modern slavery and what you can do to tackle it at Freedom United. You can also find out how to raise awareness about a wide range of human rights issues at Amnesty International.

www.freedomunited.org/about-us
www.amnesty.org/en/what-we-do

4 Vote!

When you become an adult, one of the most powerful things you can do is vote—for politicians who promise to make life better for workers. Even now, you can write to lawmakers and tell them what issues are important to you, your family, and your community. And you can encourage the adults you know to vote!

5 Support Trade Unions

When you enter the workforce, join a trade union if you can. You can also become involved in Amnesty International to support trade unionists who have been jailed. Check out how to take action by yourself or with your peers.

www.amnestyusa.org/take-action

Timeline

1888 Bryant & May match girls' strike takes place in the UK.

1899 Newsboys strike takes place in New York.

1904 National Child Labor Committee is founded in the United States.

1905 Industrial Workers of the World labor union is founded.

1909 Workers strike in New York shirtwaist (clothing) factories.

1911 International Women's Day is first celebrated.

1911 Triangle Shirtwaist Factory fire occurs in New York.

1919 International Labour Organization (ILO) is founded.

1919 Winnipeg General Strike— the largest in Canadian history— takes place.

1938 Employer found responsible for radium girls' deaths.

1938 U.S. Fair Labor Standards Act is passed.

1959 Steel Workers' Strike takes place.

1963 More than 250,000 demonstrators participate in the March on Washington for Jobs and Freedom.

1965 Delano grape workers' strike and grape boycott begins.

1968 Memphis Sanitation Workers' strike takes place.

1968 Dagenham Ford sewing machinists' strike takes place in the UK.

1970 Occupational Safety and Health Act is passed.

1973 Scottish engineers refuse to work on military engines from Chile to support Chilean people (UK).

1974 Health and Safety at Work Act (UK) is passed.

1977 Canadian Human Rights Act orders equal pay for women.

1980 Solidarność is formed in Poland.

1981 Canada Post workers' strike wins 17 weeks' maternity leave.

1989 Fall of the Berlin Wall brings the reunification of Germany.

1990 Solidarność wins an election landslide in Poland, and its leader Lech Walesa becomes the Polish president.

1993 Family and Medical Leave Act is passed.

2013 Rana Plaza factory collapses in Bangladesh.

2014 Fast-food workers and other low-wage workers strike.

2018 Climate activist Greta Thunberg begins school strike for the climate.

2020 Cleaning workers in Minneapolis call a strike to support the environment.

2020 Coronavirus pandemic hits workers everywhere. Unions call for better protection for essential workers and additional pay for working in dangerous conditions.

Sources

Chapter 1

"A Brief Introduction to Marxism." The Curious Classroom. August 2, 2013. https://bit.ly/33KzQtF

"History of Labour in Canada." Canadian Labour Congress. February 24, 2015. https://bit.ly/3gKgR6b

"Our Labor History Timeline." AFL-CIO. https://aflcio.org/about-us/history

Chapter 2

Domville, Stephen. "Britain: The Matchgirls' strike–from a spark to a blaze." In Defence of Marxism. July 8, 2013. https://bit.ly/2DTAnPe

Griffin, Emma. "Child Labour." British Library. May 15, 2014. https://bit.ly/2PEExNn

Moore, Kate. "The Forgotten Story Of The Radium Girls, Whose Deaths Saved Thousands Of Workers' Lives." Buzzfeed. April 4, 2019. https://bzfd.it/2PFJUMi

"Remembering the 1911 Triangle Factory Fire." Cornell University. http://trianglefire.ilr.cornell.edu

Chapter 3

Kim, Inga. "The 1965–1970 Delano Grape Strike and Boycott." United Farm Workers. March 7, 2017. https://bit.ly/2Duup7C

"Memphis Sanitation Workers' Strike." Stanford University. King Encyclopedia. https://stanford.io/3ab71HY

Nickleberry, Elmore and Taylor Rogers. "We Wanted to Be Treated as Men." Facing History and Ourselves. https://bit.ly/3isaViF

Chapter 4

"Dagenham Women's Strike." Trade Union Congress (TUC.) https://bit.ly/2DvKERT

Murray, Jessica. "Gender pay gap explained 2020." Save the Student. March 2, 2020. https://bit.ly/3ipy19C

Sefton Macdowell, Laurel. "Grace Hartman." *The Canadian Encyclopedia*. December 16, 2013. https://bit.ly/2Ebi1tc

Chapter 5

Kramer, Mark. "The Rise and Fall of Solidarity." *The New York Times*. December 12, 2011. https://nyti.ms/31A1DKM

"Poland: Solidarity Rules." *BBC News*. https://bbc.in/2CcK2Qa

Robinson, David. "World politics explainer: the end of apartheid." *The Conversation*. October 10, 2018. https://bit.ly/31FBdab

Chapter 6

"ILO Declaration on Fundamental Principles and Rights at Work." International Labour Organization. April 24, 2018. https://bit.ly/3fHKvaH

Labour Behind the Label. https://labourbehindthelabel.org/who-we-are

Thapa, Tejshree. "Remember Rana Plaza." Human Rights Watch. https://bit.ly/2DDhgci

Glossary

boycott A protest in which people refuse to buy products from or do business with an organization that is harmful

capitalism The name for a type of society where most of the money and power belongs to corporation owners and the government

carbon footprint The amount of carbon dioxide a person or organization releases

civil rights People's basic rights to be treated as equal with others and protected under the law

climate change A significant change in the world's usual climate patterns over time.

communist The name for a type of society in which money and power are shared among all members

coup A sudden, violent overthrow of a government by a small group

democratic Based on a form of government in which people elect their leader

discrimination Treating someone unfairly because they belong to a certain group

fascist A form of government that follows extreme right-wing ideas

Filipino A person who is native to the Philippine islands

globalization A trend for many aspects of life–including trade, technology, politics, and culture–to become more international

human rights Rights shared by all people, such as the right to be protected from violence, to be treated with dignity and fairness, and to have food, water, and shelter

human trafficking Buying or selling people illegally, or making money from work they are forced to do

immigrant Someone who comes to live in one country from another country

Industrial Revolution The time during the 18th and 19th centuries when machines started to be used on a huge scale

Latino A person who has Latin American heritage

martial law Rule by the military

maternity leave Time off from work that new mothers are entitled to

migrants People who move from one place to another, usually to find work

minimum wage By law, the lowest amount a worker can be paid

negotiate To discuss to agree on something, often to resolve a conflict

overtime Working for longer than your usual hours, or at different times from usual

radioactive Gives off dangerous rays or particles

refugees People who move to a new country because they are fleeing war, famine, or persecution at home

sanctions Actions, such as refusing to trade, that are taken by countries to try to affect what another country does

segregated Separated and kept apart

slavery When people are treated as property and forced to provide labor for no pay and under terrible conditions

solidarity Sticking together and standing up for each other

Soviet Connected to the Soviet Union, or USSR, a former group of states in Eurasia that included Russia

tactics A series of actions planned to achieve a particular purpose

trade unions (labor unions) Groups of workers who formally join together to negotiate about pay and working conditions

transgender When someone's gender as they experience it is different from the sex that was assigned to them at birth

welfare Financial support from the state to help people in need

Further Information

Books

Baby Professor. *The Beginnings of the Labor Unions.* Newark: Speedy Publishing, 2017.

Barghoorn, Linda. *Dolores Huerta: Advocate for Women and Workers.* New York: Crabtree Publishing, 2017.

Duncan, Alice Faye. *Memphis, Martin, and the Mountaintop: The Sanitation Strike of 1968.* New York: Boyds Mills & Kane, 2018.

Liu-Trujillo, Robert. *Dolores Huerta: Get to Know the Voice of Migrant Workers.* North Mankato: Capstone, 2020.

Margolin, Jamie. *Youth to Power: Your Voice and How to Use It.* New York: Hachette, 2020.

Marrin, Albert. *Flesh and Blood So Cheap: The Triangle Fire and Its Legacy.* New York: Random House Children's Books, 2011.

Moore, Kate. *The Radium Girls: Young Readers' Edition.* Sourcebooks Explore, 2020.

Websites

aflcio.org/about-us/history
A useful timeline of labor history in the United States.

www.bl.uk/sisterhood/themes/equality-and-work
A page linking to articles about women's fight for workplace equality in the UK.

www.ilo.org/global/about-the-ilo/history/lang--en/index.htm
A detailed source of information about the history of the International Labour Organization (ILO).

kinginstitute.stanford.edu/encyclopedia/march-washington-jobs-and-freedom
Find out about the March on Washington for Jobs and Freedom—and much more—in Stanford University's King Encyclopedia.

www.thecanadianencyclopedia.ca/en/article/working-class-history
A detailed account of the history of the working class and the labor movement in Canada from *The Canadian Encyclopedia*.

trianglefire.ilr.cornell.edu
A fascinating source of information on the Triangle Shirtwaist Fire, including interviews with survivors and witnesses.

Index